Mighty Mummies

Haydn Middleton

Mummy's The Word

How would you like to live forever? Long ago, in a land called Egypt, people thought you could! It didn't matter if you died on earth. You could then go and live in a kind of holiday world! But you would still need your body. So, people worked on your dead body and made sure it did not turn to dust. They made you into ... a **mummy!**

As you travel through these pages, write down and keep your answers to each **QUIZ** question. (Remember, the answers are in the book!) Ok? On with the Mummbo Jummbo!

What's in Store?

Making a Mummy

How to make sure your mummy will live forever

PAGES 6 TO 9

Where the most important mummies got to hang out!

PAGES 10 TO 13

Mummy Homes

Mummy Surprise!

Be afraid! Be very afraid before turning to ...

PAGES 14 TO 15

Back From the Dead

How some mummies showed up again, years later ...

PAGES 16 TO 19

Mummy Secrets

What mummies from thousands of years ago can tell us today

PAGES 20 TO 23

Making a Mummy

DAY 1

Cut the body open and take out most of the insides. Use a hook to pull out the brain … through the nose! Store all the bits in big painted jars BUT wrap up the heart and put it to one side.

DAY 2

Give the body a good wash, using wine or vinegar. Then dry it out by packing it in special salt. Leave to stand (or lie!) for 40 days.

DAY 42

Stuff the dried-out body with cloth. Carefully put the heart back inside too. Then rub all sorts of lotions into the body. This will stop the skin from cracking.

DAY 70

Wrap the body, from head to toe, in bandages. Place some little lucky charms between the layers. Then paint a face mask showing what the dead person looked like – or maybe a bit more handsome than that!

The finished mummy was put in a case. This case was the same shape as the mummy inside, with a face painted on. Then a holy man wearing a dog mask came along. He touched the eyes, ears and mouth, as if he was casting a spell. Now the mummy would be able to see, hear and speak in the place it was going to. What place was that? Read the next section to find out!

Only rich dead people had such cool mummy cases. Some got more than one case – each fitted inside the other!

8 **QUIZ**   People wrapping up a mummy put little

Feline Fact

The people of Egypt thought animals like cows, crocodiles and snakes brought good luck. Best of all were cats. When their cats died, people often made them into mummies.

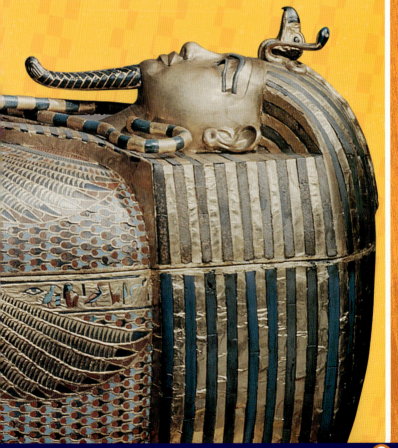

****** for luck in among the bandages.

Mummy Homes

The mummies of rich people were put in big stone homes called tombs. Mummies of poor people were just buried in holes in the desert! The richest people in Egypt were the kings. They were called pharaohs (say 'fair-ohs'). The pharaohs' tombs were massive. The most famous tombs were the pyramids.

Pharaoh Khufu's pyramid is made of about 2.3 million blocks of stone and is almost 150m high.

Around 5000 years ago, Pharaoh Khufu (say 'koo-foo') got thousands of workers to build the biggest pyramid of all. When he died, his people took his mummy there. They carried the mummy down spooky long corridors and then left it in a special little room in the middle.

FLeSH-eaTeR FaCT

Khufu's mummy was left in a stone box called a sarcophagus (say 'sar-coff-a-guss'). This weird word means … flesh-eater.

Mummies were NOT really dead!

12 QUIZ People believed that after they died, they travelle

Well, that's what people in Egypt believed!

They thought mummies inside their tombs went on to new lives. Pharaoh mummies went to live in the sky. Ordinary mummies travelled to a kind of holiday world: the Field of Reeds. People wanted to give them presents for the journey. They thought mummies would need:

*Sometimes real live servants were killed and buried alongside their pharaohs!

from their home country of ***** to the Field of *****.

Mummy Surprise!

People in Egypt believed that if you broke into a mummy's tomb to steal all the precious things, the mummy would curse you. Do not disturb this mummy or the deadly curse will get YOU!

Back From the Dead

Some mummies' tombs had huge amounts of treasure inside. This was too tempting for many thieves. They dug tunnels to get inside, or bribed the guards to let them in. Then they stole whatever they could carry. The people of Egypt tried to stop these raids by building huge stone guardians for the tombs. One of these guardians was called the Sphinx.

But the Sphinx didn't frighten off many thieves. And it was no good at chasing them away! All the pyramids were robbed of their treasure.

The thieves even took mummies from the pyramids. WHAT FOR? People used to turn mummies into powder. Then they sold it as a magical kind of medicine.

The Sphinx

False Beard Fact

How did the scientists know Tutankhamun was once a pharaoh? The face masks of rulers had false beards. This was a sign that they were once pharaohs.

Bug!

Experts thought that all the big, rich tombs had been robbed. They were wrong. About 100 years ago, scientists found a secret tomb, hidden deep inside a rock. There were thousands of precious objects inside: statues, thrones, weapons, musical instruments and jewellery. There was also a coffin. It contained the mummy of a young pharaoh. He ruled more than 3000 years ago and his name was …

TUTANKHAMUN

QUIZ   The ****** was big and strong-looking, bu

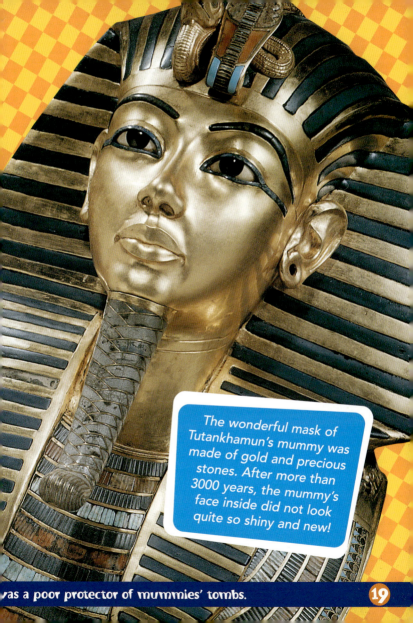

The wonderful mask of Tutankhamun's mummy was made of gold and precious stones. After more than 3000 years, the mummy's face inside did not look quite so shiny and new!

vas a poor protector of mummies' tombs.

Mummy Secrets

Mummies cannot speak!

FaMiLY FaCT

Every living thing contains DNA. People who are related to each other have similar DNA. Scientists sometimes find mummies with similar DNA. They were related!

But we still know their secrets.

How? In the past, scientists used to unwrap mummies. Today, scientists use machines to take a 3D picture of a mummy's insides. There may be something in the mummy's stomach. If there is, the picture shows the last thing the person ate. Scientists can also do tests on bits of a mummy's skin and bone. This helps them work out what germs the person once had.

A mummy's teeth tell scientists things too. They show what kind of food the person usually ate – and if he or she looked after them properly!

Scientists can learn a mummy's secrets from its tomb. The tombs of rich people were like little houses, with paintings on the inside walls.

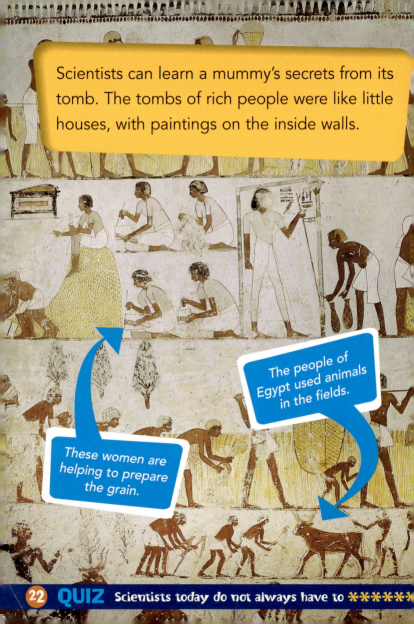

These women are helping to prepare the grain.

The people of Egypt used animals in the fields.

22 QUIZ Scientists today do not always have to ✶✶✶✶✶✶